50 Australian Outback Cooking Recipes for Home

By: Kelly Johnson

Table of Contents

- Lemon Myrtle and Macadamia Crusted Snapper
- Bush Tomato and Pepperberry Kangaroo Sausages
- Crocodile Tail Soup with Lemon Myrtle Dumplings
- Kangaroo and Bush Tomato Lasagna
- Lemon Myrtle and Pepperberry Crusted Tuna Steak
- Bush Tomato and Quandong Chutney
- Emu Egg Benedict with Pepperberry Hollandaise
- Grilled Barramundi with Bush Tomato Salsa
- Lemon Myrtle and Wattleseed Ice Cream
- Bush Tomato and Pepperberry Chocolate Brownies

Kangaroo Steak with Bush Tomato Relish

Ingredients:

For the Kangaroo Steak:

- 4 kangaroo steaks
- Salt and pepper to taste
- Olive oil for cooking

For the Bush Tomato Relish:

- 1 cup bush tomatoes (also known as desert tomatoes or kutjera)
- 1 small onion, finely chopped
- 2 cloves garlic, minced
- 1 tablespoon balsamic vinegar
- 1 tablespoon honey
- Salt and pepper to taste

Instructions:

1. Begin by preparing the bush tomato relish. In a small saucepan, heat some olive oil over medium heat.
2. Add the finely chopped onion and minced garlic to the saucepan. Cook until the onion becomes translucent, stirring occasionally.
3. Once the onion is cooked, add the bush tomatoes to the saucepan. Allow them to cook down until they start to soften and release their juices, about 5-7 minutes.
4. Stir in the balsamic vinegar and honey, and season with salt and pepper to taste. Continue to cook for another 5 minutes, or until the relish thickens slightly. Remove from heat and set aside.
5. Meanwhile, season the kangaroo steaks with salt and pepper on both sides.
6. Heat a grill pan or skillet over medium-high heat and add a drizzle of olive oil.
7. Once the pan is hot, add the kangaroo steaks and cook for 2-3 minutes on each side for medium-rare, or longer if you prefer your steak more well-done.
8. Once the steaks are cooked to your desired doneness, remove them from the pan and let them rest for a few minutes.
9. Serve the kangaroo steaks hot, topped with the bush tomato relish.
10. Enjoy your Kangaroo Steak with Bush Tomato Relish!

Emu Kebabs with Lemon Myrtle Marinade

Ingredients:

For the Emu Kebabs:

- 500g emu meat, cubed
- 1 red bell pepper, cut into chunks
- 1 green bell pepper, cut into chunks
- 1 red onion, cut into chunks
- Wooden or metal skewers

For the Lemon Myrtle Marinade:

- 2 tablespoons lemon myrtle leaves, finely chopped
- 1/4 cup olive oil
- 2 tablespoons lemon juice
- 2 cloves garlic, minced
- 1 teaspoon honey
- Salt and pepper to taste

Instructions:

1. In a small bowl, combine the finely chopped lemon myrtle leaves, olive oil, lemon juice, minced garlic, honey, salt, and pepper. Mix well to combine.
2. Place the cubed emu meat in a shallow dish or resealable plastic bag. Pour the lemon myrtle marinade over the emu meat, making sure it is evenly coated. Cover the dish or seal the bag, then refrigerate for at least 2 hours, or preferably overnight, to allow the flavors to develop.
3. If you're using wooden skewers, soak them in water for about 30 minutes to prevent them from burning during cooking.
4. Preheat your grill or barbecue to medium-high heat.
5. While the grill is heating up, prepare the skewers by threading the marinated emu meat, red bell pepper chunks, green bell pepper chunks, and red onion chunks onto the skewers, alternating the ingredients.
6. Once the grill is hot, place the emu kebabs on the grill and cook for about 3-4 minutes per side, or until the meat is cooked to your desired level of doneness and the vegetables are tender and slightly charred.
7. Once cooked, remove the emu kebabs from the grill and transfer them to a serving platter.
8. Serve the emu kebabs hot, garnished with some extra lemon myrtle leaves if desired.
9. Enjoy your Emu Kebabs with Lemon Myrtle Marinade!

Crocodile Sausage Rolls

Ingredients:

For the Crocodile Sausage Filling:

- 500g crocodile meat, minced
- 1 small onion, finely chopped
- 2 cloves garlic, minced
- 1/4 cup breadcrumbs
- 1 egg
- 1 tablespoon Worcestershire sauce
- 1 teaspoon dried mixed herbs (such as thyme, oregano, and rosemary)
- Salt and pepper to taste

For the Pastry:

- 2 sheets puff pastry, thawed if frozen
- 1 egg, beaten (for egg wash)

Instructions:

1. Preheat your oven to 200°C (390°F) and line a baking tray with parchment paper.
2. In a large mixing bowl, combine the minced crocodile meat, finely chopped onion, minced garlic, breadcrumbs, egg, Worcestershire sauce, dried mixed herbs, salt, and pepper. Mix well until all ingredients are evenly incorporated.
3. Lay out the thawed puff pastry sheets on a clean work surface. Cut each sheet in half lengthwise to create four long strips.
4. Divide the crocodile sausage filling into four equal portions. Shape each portion into a long sausage shape and place it along the length of each pastry strip.
5. Roll the pastry around the filling, enclosing it completely. Seal the edges by pressing them together with your fingers.
6. Cut each long sausage roll into smaller pieces, about 5-6 cm (2-2.5 inches) in length.
7. Place the mini crocodile sausage rolls onto the prepared baking tray, seam side down. Leave some space between each roll to allow for expansion during baking.
8. Brush the tops of the sausage rolls with beaten egg to give them a golden finish when baked.
9. Bake the crocodile sausage rolls in the preheated oven for 20-25 minutes, or until the pastry is puffed and golden brown, and the filling is cooked through.
10. Once baked, remove the crocodile sausage rolls from the oven and transfer them to a wire rack to cool slightly before serving.

11. Serve the crocodile sausage rolls warm as a delicious appetizer or snack.
12. Enjoy your Crocodile Sausage Rolls!

Grilled Barramundi with Macadamia Pesto

Ingredients:

For the Grilled Barramundi:

- 4 barramundi fillets (about 150g each)
- Salt and pepper to taste
- Olive oil for brushing

For the Macadamia Pesto:

- 1 cup fresh basil leaves
- 1/2 cup macadamia nuts
- 2 cloves garlic, peeled
- 1/4 cup grated Parmesan cheese
- 1/4 cup olive oil
- Salt and pepper to taste
- Juice of 1/2 lemon (optional)

Instructions:

1. Preheat your grill to medium-high heat.
2. Season the barramundi fillets with salt and pepper on both sides.
3. Brush the grill grates with olive oil to prevent sticking.
4. Place the barramundi fillets on the preheated grill and cook for 3-4 minutes per side, or until the fish is cooked through and flakes easily with a fork. Cooking time will depend on the thickness of the fillets.
5. While the barramundi is grilling, prepare the macadamia pesto. In a food processor, combine the fresh basil leaves, macadamia nuts, garlic cloves, grated Parmesan cheese, and olive oil. Pulse until the mixture forms a coarse paste.
6. Season the pesto with salt and pepper to taste. If desired, add the juice of half a lemon for a hint of acidity.
7. Once the barramundi fillets are cooked, remove them from the grill and transfer them to a serving platter.
8. Spoon the macadamia pesto over the grilled barramundi fillets, spreading it evenly.
9. Serve the Grilled Barramundi with Macadamia Pesto immediately, garnished with additional basil leaves if desired.
10. Enjoy your delicious and flavorful Grilled Barramundi with Macadamia Pesto!

Outback Lamb Stew with Wild Herbs

Ingredients:

- 1 kg lamb stew meat, cut into chunks
- 2 tablespoons olive oil
- 1 onion, chopped
- 2 cloves garlic, minced
- 2 carrots, peeled and diced
- 2 potatoes, peeled and diced
- 2 cups beef or lamb broth
- 1 cup red wine (optional)
- 2 tablespoons tomato paste
- 1 teaspoon dried thyme
- 1 teaspoon dried rosemary
- 1 teaspoon dried oregano
- Salt and pepper to taste
- Fresh wild herbs (such as lemon myrtle, warrigal greens, or bush tomatoes) for garnish

Instructions:

1. Heat the olive oil in a large pot or Dutch oven over medium-high heat.
2. Add the chopped onion and minced garlic to the pot, and sauté until softened and fragrant, about 2-3 minutes.
3. Add the lamb stew meat to the pot, and cook until browned on all sides, about 5-7 minutes.
4. Once the lamb is browned, add the diced carrots and potatoes to the pot, and stir to combine.
5. Pour in the beef or lamb broth and red wine (if using), and stir in the tomato paste, dried thyme, dried rosemary, and dried oregano. Season with salt and pepper to taste.
6. Bring the stew to a simmer, then reduce the heat to low. Cover the pot with a lid, and let the stew simmer gently for 1.5 to 2 hours, or until the lamb is tender and the vegetables are cooked through.
7. Once the stew is cooked, taste and adjust the seasoning if necessary.
8. Serve the Outback Lamb Stew hot, garnished with fresh wild herbs such as lemon myrtle, warrigal greens, or bush tomatoes.

9. Enjoy your hearty and flavorful Outback Lamb Stew with Wild Herbs!

Bush Tomato Damper Bread

Ingredients:

- 2 cups self-raising flour
- 1/2 teaspoon salt
- 1 tablespoon dried bush tomatoes, chopped
- 1/4 cup butter, cold and diced
- 3/4 cup milk
- Extra flour for dusting

Instructions:

1. Preheat your oven to 200°C (400°F). Line a baking tray with parchment paper or grease it lightly with butter.
2. In a large mixing bowl, sift the self-raising flour and salt together.
3. Add the chopped dried bush tomatoes to the flour mixture and stir to combine.
4. Using your fingertips, rub the cold, diced butter into the flour mixture until it resembles coarse breadcrumbs.
5. Make a well in the center of the flour mixture and pour in the milk. Use a flat-bladed knife or a spatula to mix the ingredients together until a soft dough forms. Be careful not to overmix.
6. Turn the dough out onto a lightly floured surface and knead it gently for 1-2 minutes until it comes together into a smooth ball.
7. Shape the dough into a round loaf and place it onto the prepared baking tray.
8. Use a sharp knife to score a cross or X on the top of the loaf, about 1 cm deep.
9. Bake the Bush Tomato Damper Bread in the preheated oven for 25-30 minutes, or until it is golden brown and sounds hollow when tapped on the bottom.
10. Once baked, transfer the damper bread to a wire rack to cool slightly before serving.
11. Serve the Bush Tomato Damper Bread warm or at room temperature, sliced and spread with butter or your favorite toppings.
12. Enjoy your delicious and rustic Bush Tomato Damper Bread!

Lemon Myrtle Chicken Skewers

Ingredients:

For the Chicken Skewers:

- 500g chicken breast, cut into cubes
- Wooden skewers, soaked in water for at least 30 minutes

For the Lemon Myrtle Marinade:

- 2 tablespoons lemon myrtle leaves, finely chopped
- 1/4 cup olive oil
- 2 tablespoons lemon juice
- 2 cloves garlic, minced
- 1 teaspoon honey
- Salt and pepper to taste

Instructions:

1. In a small bowl, combine the finely chopped lemon myrtle leaves, olive oil, lemon juice, minced garlic, honey, salt, and pepper. Mix well to combine.
2. Place the chicken breast cubes in a shallow dish or resealable plastic bag. Pour the lemon myrtle marinade over the chicken, making sure it is evenly coated. Cover the dish or seal the bag, then refrigerate for at least 2 hours, or preferably overnight, to allow the flavors to develop.
3. Once the chicken has marinated, thread the chicken cubes onto the soaked wooden skewers, dividing them evenly among the skewers.
4. Preheat your grill or barbecue to medium-high heat.
5. Brush the grill grates with oil to prevent sticking.
6. Place the chicken skewers on the preheated grill and cook for 4-5 minutes on each side, or until the chicken is cooked through and has nice grill marks.
7. Once the chicken skewers are cooked, remove them from the grill and transfer them to a serving platter.
8. Serve the Lemon Myrtle Chicken Skewers hot, garnished with some extra lemon myrtle leaves if desired.
9. Enjoy your flavorful and aromatic Lemon Myrtle Chicken Skewers!

Saltbush and Pepperberry Kangaroo Jerky

Ingredients:

- 500g kangaroo meat (either fillets or steaks)
- 2 tablespoons saltbush leaves
- 1 tablespoon ground pepperberry
- 2 tablespoons soy sauce
- 1 tablespoon Worcestershire sauce
- 1 tablespoon honey
- 1 teaspoon garlic powder
- 1 teaspoon onion powder
- 1 teaspoon smoked paprika (optional, for added flavor)
- 1/2 teaspoon ground black pepper

Instructions:

1. Slice the kangaroo meat into thin strips, about 1/4 inch thick. It's easier to slice thinly if the meat is slightly frozen.
2. In a bowl, mix together the saltbush leaves, ground pepperberry, soy sauce, Worcestershire sauce, honey, garlic powder, onion powder, smoked paprika (if using), and ground black pepper to create the marinade.
3. Place the kangaroo meat strips in a shallow dish or resealable plastic bag. Pour the marinade over the meat, making sure each piece is well coated. Marinate in the refrigerator for at least 4 hours, or overnight for best results.
4. Preheat your oven to its lowest setting, usually around 80-100°C (175-200°F).
5. Remove the marinated kangaroo meat from the refrigerator and drain off any excess marinade.
6. Arrange the kangaroo strips on a wire rack placed over a baking tray to catch any drips.
7. Place the wire rack with the kangaroo strips in the preheated oven and prop the oven door open slightly to allow air circulation. This helps to dehydrate the meat.
8. Dry the kangaroo jerky in the oven for 4-6 hours, or until it is firm and dry to the touch. Check it periodically and rotate the trays if necessary for even drying.
9. Once the kangaroo jerky is dried to your liking, remove it from the oven and let it cool completely.
10. Store the kangaroo jerky in an airtight container or ziplock bags at room temperature for up to a week. For longer storage, refrigerate or freeze it.
11. Enjoy your homemade Saltbush and Pepperberry Kangaroo Jerky as a tasty and nutritious snack!

Wattleseed Anzac Biscuits

Ingredients:

- 1 cup rolled oats
- 1 cup desiccated coconut
- 1 cup all-purpose flour
- 1/2 cup wattleseed (roasted and ground)
- 3/4 cup brown sugar
- 125g unsalted butter
- 2 tablespoons golden syrup
- 1 teaspoon bicarbonate of soda
- 2 tablespoons boiling water

Instructions:

1. Preheat your oven to 160°C (320°F). Line baking trays with parchment paper.
2. In a large mixing bowl, combine the rolled oats, desiccated coconut, all-purpose flour, wattleseed, and brown sugar. Mix well to combine.
3. In a small saucepan, melt the butter and golden syrup together over low heat, stirring until smooth.
4. In a small bowl, mix the bicarbonate of soda with the boiling water until dissolved.
5. Add the bicarbonate of soda mixture to the melted butter and golden syrup mixture. It will foam up slightly.
6. Pour the wet mixture into the dry ingredients and stir until well combined and the mixture forms a dough.
7. Roll tablespoons of the dough into balls and place them on the prepared baking trays, leaving some space between each ball for spreading.
8. Flatten each ball slightly with the back of a spoon or your fingers.
9. Bake the biscuits in the preheated oven for 12-15 minutes, or until golden brown.
10. Remove the biscuits from the oven and allow them to cool on the baking trays for a few minutes before transferring them to a wire rack to cool completely.
11. Once cooled, store the Wattleseed Anzac Biscuits in an airtight container at room temperature for up to a week.
12. Enjoy these delicious biscuits with a cup of tea or coffee, savoring the unique flavor of wattleseed in every bite!

Bush Tomato and Cheddar Scones

Ingredients:

- 2 cups all-purpose flour
- 1 tablespoon baking powder
- 1/2 teaspoon salt
- 1/4 cup cold unsalted butter, cubed
- 1/2 cup grated cheddar cheese
- 2 tablespoons chopped dried bush tomatoes
- 1/2 cup milk, plus extra for brushing

Instructions:

1. Preheat your oven to 200°C (400°F). Line a baking sheet with parchment paper or lightly grease it.
2. In a large mixing bowl, whisk together the all-purpose flour, baking powder, and salt.
3. Add the cold cubed butter to the flour mixture. Using your fingertips or a pastry cutter, work the butter into the flour until the mixture resembles coarse crumbs with pea-sized pieces of butter remaining.
4. Stir in the grated cheddar cheese and chopped dried bush tomatoes until evenly distributed.
5. Make a well in the center of the mixture and pour in the milk. Use a fork or a spatula to gently mix until a soft dough forms. Be careful not to overmix.
6. Turn the dough out onto a lightly floured surface. Gently knead the dough a few times until it comes together, but avoid overworking it.
7. Pat the dough into a circle about 1 inch (2.5 cm) thick. Use a floured round cutter (about 2 inches in diameter) to cut out scones from the dough. Gather any scraps, gently pat them together, and cut out more scones until all the dough is used.
8. Place the scones on the prepared baking sheet, leaving some space between each one. Brush the tops of the scones with a little milk to help them brown.
9. Bake in the preheated oven for 12-15 minutes, or until the scones are golden brown and cooked through.
10. Remove the scones from the oven and transfer them to a wire rack to cool slightly.
11. Serve the Bush Tomato and Cheddar Scones warm with butter or your favorite spreads.
12. Enjoy these savory scones as a delicious snack or accompaniment to soups and salads!

Grilled Crocodile Tail with Bush Spices

Ingredients:

- 1 crocodile tail, skin removed and cleaned (approximately 1-2 kg)
- 2 tablespoons olive oil
- 2 cloves garlic, minced
- 1 tablespoon lemon juice
- 1 teaspoon ground wattleseed
- 1 teaspoon ground pepperberry
- 1 teaspoon ground bush tomato
- Salt and pepper to taste

Instructions:

1. Preheat your grill to medium-high heat.
2. In a small bowl, combine the olive oil, minced garlic, lemon juice, ground wattleseed, ground pepperberry, and ground bush tomato. Mix well to form a marinade.
3. Pat the crocodile tail dry with paper towels. Score the flesh of the crocodile tail with a sharp knife, making shallow cuts diagonally across the surface. This will help the marinade penetrate the meat.
4. Rub the marinade all over the crocodile tail, making sure to coat it evenly. Season with salt and pepper to taste.
5. Place the marinated crocodile tail on the preheated grill. Cook for approximately 10-15 minutes per side, depending on the thickness of the tail, or until the meat is cooked through and tender.
6. While grilling, baste the crocodile tail with any remaining marinade to keep it moist and flavorful.
7. Once cooked, remove the crocodile tail from the grill and transfer it to a cutting board. Allow it to rest for a few minutes before slicing.
8. Slice the grilled crocodile tail into serving portions and arrange them on a platter.
9. Serve the grilled crocodile tail with bush spices hot, garnished with lemon wedges and fresh herbs if desired.
10. Enjoy this unique and delicious dish as a showcase of Australian flavors!

Spinach and Warrigal Greens Quiche

Ingredients:

For the crust:

- 1 1/4 cups all-purpose flour
- 1/2 teaspoon salt
- 1/2 cup unsalted butter, cold and diced
- 3-4 tablespoons ice water

For the filling:

- 1 tablespoon olive oil
- 1 onion, finely chopped
- 2 cloves garlic, minced
- 200g fresh spinach, washed and chopped
- 200g warrigal greens, washed and chopped
- 4 eggs
- 1 cup milk
- 1 cup grated cheddar cheese
- Salt and pepper to taste
- Pinch of nutmeg (optional)

Instructions:

1. Preheat your oven to 180°C (350°F).
2. To make the crust, in a food processor, combine the all-purpose flour and salt. Add the cold diced butter and pulse until the mixture resembles coarse crumbs.
3. Gradually add the ice water, one tablespoon at a time, and pulse until the dough comes together. Be careful not to overmix.
4. Transfer the dough to a floured surface and shape it into a disk. Wrap it in plastic wrap and refrigerate for at least 30 minutes.
5. Roll out the chilled dough on a floured surface to fit a 9-inch pie dish. Press the dough into the pie dish and trim any excess from the edges. Prick the bottom of the crust with a fork.
6. Line the crust with parchment paper and fill it with pie weights or dried beans. Blind bake the crust in the preheated oven for 15 minutes. Remove the parchment paper and weights, and bake for an additional 5 minutes, or until the crust is lightly golden. Set aside to cool.
7. In a skillet, heat the olive oil over medium heat. Add the chopped onion and minced garlic, and cook until softened and fragrant, about 3-4 minutes.

8. Add the chopped spinach and warrigal greens to the skillet. Cook until wilted and any excess moisture has evaporated, about 5 minutes. Remove from heat and let cool slightly.
9. In a separate bowl, whisk together the eggs and milk. Stir in the grated cheddar cheese and cooked spinach-warrigal greens mixture. Season with salt, pepper, and a pinch of nutmeg, if using.
10. Pour the filling into the pre-baked pie crust.
11. Bake the quiche in the preheated oven for 35-40 minutes, or until the filling is set and the top is golden brown.
12. Remove the quiche from the oven and let it cool for a few minutes before slicing and serving.
13. Enjoy your Spinach and Warrigal Greens Quiche warm or at room temperature, as a delicious meal or snack!

Wallaby Burgers with Outback BBQ Sauce

Ingredients:

For the Wallaby Patties:

- 500g ground wallaby meat
- 1 small onion, finely chopped
- 2 cloves garlic, minced
- 1/4 cup breadcrumbs
- 1 egg
- Salt and pepper to taste
- Olive oil for cooking

For the Outback BBQ Sauce:

- 1 cup ketchup
- 2 tablespoons Worcestershire sauce
- 2 tablespoons apple cider vinegar
- 2 tablespoons brown sugar
- 1 teaspoon smoked paprika
- 1 teaspoon garlic powder
- 1/2 teaspoon onion powder
- Salt and pepper to taste

For assembling the burgers:

- Burger buns
- Lettuce leaves
- Tomato slices
- Red onion slices
- Cheese slices (optional)

Instructions:

1. In a large mixing bowl, combine the ground wallaby meat, finely chopped onion, minced garlic, breadcrumbs, egg, salt, and pepper. Mix well until all ingredients are evenly incorporated.
2. Divide the mixture into equal portions and shape them into burger patties.

3. Heat some olive oil in a skillet or grill pan over medium-high heat. Cook the wallaby patties for 4-5 minutes on each side, or until cooked through and nicely browned. Make sure the patties reach an internal temperature of 160°F (71°C).
4. While the patties are cooking, prepare the Outback BBQ sauce. In a small saucepan, combine the ketchup, Worcestershire sauce, apple cider vinegar, brown sugar, smoked paprika, garlic powder, onion powder, salt, and pepper. Stir well to combine.
5. Bring the sauce to a simmer over medium heat, then reduce the heat to low and let it cook for about 10-15 minutes, stirring occasionally, until it thickens slightly.
6. Once the wallaby patties are cooked and the BBQ sauce is ready, assemble the burgers. Toast the burger buns if desired, then place a lettuce leaf on the bottom half of each bun, followed by a wallaby patty.
7. Spoon some Outback BBQ sauce over the wallaby patty, then add tomato slices, red onion slices, and cheese slices if using.
8. Top with the other half of the burger bun and serve immediately.
9. Enjoy your delicious Wallaby Burgers with Outback BBQ Sauce, accompanied by your favorite sides!

Witchetty Grub Stir-Fry

Ingredients:

- 250g witchetty grubs
- 2 tablespoons vegetable oil
- 1 onion, sliced
- 2 cloves garlic, minced
- 1 red bell pepper, sliced
- 1 green bell pepper, sliced
- 1 carrot, julienned
- 1 zucchini, sliced
- 200g snow peas, trimmed
- 2 tablespoons soy sauce
- 1 tablespoon oyster sauce
- 1 teaspoon sesame oil
- Salt and pepper to taste
- Cooked rice or noodles, for serving

Instructions:

1. Prepare the witchetty grubs by blanching them in boiling water for 2-3 minutes. Drain and set aside.
2. Heat the vegetable oil in a large skillet or wok over high heat.
3. Add the sliced onion and minced garlic to the skillet. Stir-fry for 1-2 minutes until fragrant.
4. Add the blanched witchetty grubs to the skillet. Stir-fry for another 2-3 minutes until they start to turn golden brown.
5. Add the sliced red and green bell peppers, julienned carrot, sliced zucchini, and trimmed snow peas to the skillet. Stir-fry for 3-4 minutes until the vegetables are tender-crisp.
6. In a small bowl, mix together the soy sauce, oyster sauce, and sesame oil. Pour the sauce over the stir-fry and toss to coat evenly.
7. Season with salt and pepper to taste.
8. Continue to stir-fry for another 1-2 minutes until everything is heated through and well combined.
9. Remove the stir-fry from the heat and serve immediately with cooked rice or noodles.
10. Enjoy your adventurous Witchetty Grub Stir-Fry!

Bush Tomato and Pepperberry Chicken Wings

Ingredients:

For the Chicken Wings:

- 1 kg chicken wings
- Salt and pepper to taste
- Olive oil for brushing

For the Bush Tomato and Pepperberry Marinade:

- 2 tablespoons bush tomato paste
- 1 tablespoon ground pepperberry
- 2 tablespoons olive oil
- 2 cloves garlic, minced
- 1 tablespoon honey
- Juice of 1 lemon
- Salt to taste

Instructions:

1. Preheat your oven to 200°C (400°F).
2. Pat the chicken wings dry with paper towels and season them with salt and pepper.
3. In a bowl, combine the bush tomato paste, ground pepperberry, olive oil, minced garlic, honey, lemon juice, and salt. Mix well to form a marinade.
4. Place the chicken wings in a large resealable plastic bag or a shallow dish. Pour the marinade over the chicken wings, making sure they are evenly coated. Seal the bag or cover the dish, and refrigerate for at least 30 minutes, or preferably overnight, to allow the flavors to meld.
5. Remove the marinated chicken wings from the refrigerator and let them come to room temperature for about 15 minutes.
6. Line a baking sheet with parchment paper or aluminum foil for easy cleanup. Place a wire rack on top of the baking sheet.
7. Arrange the chicken wings on the wire rack in a single layer, leaving a little space between each wing.
8. Brush the chicken wings with a little olive oil to help them crisp up in the oven.
9. Bake the chicken wings in the preheated oven for 35-40 minutes, or until they are cooked through and golden brown, flipping halfway through cooking.

10. Once cooked, remove the chicken wings from the oven and let them rest for a few minutes before serving.
11. Serve the Bush Tomato and Pepperberry Chicken Wings hot, garnished with some fresh herbs if desired.
12. Enjoy your flavorful and aromatic chicken wings with a unique Australian twist!

Lemon Myrtle and Honey Glazed Pork Ribs

Ingredients:

For the Pork Ribs:

- 1 rack of pork ribs
- Salt and pepper to taste
- Olive oil for brushing

For the Glaze:

- 1/4 cup honey
- 2 tablespoons lemon myrtle leaves, finely chopped
- 2 tablespoons soy sauce
- 2 cloves garlic, minced
- 1 tablespoon apple cider vinegar
- 1 teaspoon Dijon mustard
- 1/2 teaspoon ground ginger
- 1/4 teaspoon red pepper flakes (optional, for added heat)

Instructions:

1. Preheat your oven to 160°C (325°F).
2. Prepare the pork ribs by removing the membrane from the back of the rack, if present. Season the ribs generously with salt and pepper on both sides.
3. Place the seasoned ribs on a baking sheet lined with aluminum foil or parchment paper.
4. Brush the ribs with olive oil to help them brown and keep them moist during cooking.
5. In a small saucepan, combine the honey, chopped lemon myrtle leaves, soy sauce, minced garlic, apple cider vinegar, Dijon mustard, ground ginger, and red pepper flakes (if using). Stir well to combine.
6. Place the saucepan over medium heat and bring the glaze mixture to a simmer. Let it cook for 2-3 minutes, stirring occasionally, until slightly thickened.
7. Pour half of the glaze over the pork ribs, brushing it evenly to coat both sides.
8. Cover the ribs loosely with aluminum foil and bake in the preheated oven for 1.5 to 2 hours, or until the meat is tender and begins to pull away from the bones.
9. Remove the foil from the ribs and brush them with the remaining glaze. Increase the oven temperature to 200°C (400°F) and bake for an additional 10-15 minutes, or until the glaze is caramelized and sticky.

10. Once cooked, remove the ribs from the oven and let them rest for a few minutes before slicing.
11. Serve the Lemon Myrtle and Honey Glazed Pork Ribs hot, garnished with additional chopped lemon myrtle leaves if desired.
12. Enjoy your delicious and flavorful pork ribs with a unique Australian twist!

Emu Egg Omelette with Bush Chutney

Ingredients:

For the Emu Egg Omelette:

- 1 emu egg (or equivalent amount of chicken eggs)
- Salt and pepper to taste
- 1 tablespoon butter or olive oil
- Optional fillings: diced vegetables, cooked meats, grated cheese

For the Bush Chutney:

- 1 cup mixed bush fruits (such as quandongs, muntries, or Davidson plums), chopped
- 1 onion, finely chopped
- 2 cloves garlic, minced
- 1 tablespoon olive oil
- 2 tablespoons apple cider vinegar
- 2 tablespoons honey or sugar
- Salt and pepper to taste

Instructions:

1. To make the Bush Chutney, heat olive oil in a saucepan over medium heat. Add the chopped onion and minced garlic, and cook until softened and fragrant, about 3-4 minutes.
2. Add the chopped mixed bush fruits to the saucepan. Cook, stirring occasionally, until the fruits start to soften, about 5-7 minutes.
3. Stir in the apple cider vinegar and honey (or sugar). Season with salt and pepper to taste. Continue to cook for another 5-10 minutes, or until the chutney thickens slightly. Remove from heat and let it cool.
4. For the Emu Egg Omelette, crack the emu egg into a bowl and whisk it until well beaten. Season with salt and pepper to taste.
5. Heat butter or olive oil in a non-stick skillet over medium heat. Pour the beaten emu egg into the skillet, tilting the pan to spread the egg evenly.
6. Cook the omelette for 2-3 minutes, or until the edges start to set and the bottom is golden brown.
7. If using fillings, sprinkle them over one half of the omelette.
8. Using a spatula, gently fold the other half of the omelette over the fillings. Cook for another 1-2 minutes, or until the omelette is cooked through and the fillings are heated.

9. Slide the omelette onto a plate and serve hot, accompanied by a dollop of bush chutney on the side.

10. Enjoy your flavorful Emu Egg Omelette with Bush Chutney, a unique and delicious Australian breakfast dish!

Kangaroo and Bush Tomato Pasta

Ingredients:

- 250g kangaroo meat, thinly sliced
- 250g pasta (such as spaghetti or fettuccine)
- 2 tablespoons olive oil
- 1 onion, finely chopped
- 2 cloves garlic, minced
- 1/4 cup dried bush tomatoes, chopped
- 1 can (400g) diced tomatoes
- 1 teaspoon dried mixed herbs (such as thyme, oregano, and basil)
- Salt and pepper to taste
- Grated Parmesan cheese for serving
- Fresh basil leaves for garnish (optional)

Instructions:

1. Cook the pasta according to the package instructions until al dente. Drain and set aside.
2. Heat 1 tablespoon of olive oil in a large skillet over medium-high heat. Add the thinly sliced kangaroo meat and cook for 3-4 minutes, or until browned and cooked through. Remove the kangaroo meat from the skillet and set aside.
3. In the same skillet, heat the remaining tablespoon of olive oil. Add the chopped onion and minced garlic, and sauté until softened and fragrant, about 2-3 minutes.
4. Stir in the dried bush tomatoes and cook for another minute.
5. Add the diced tomatoes (with their juices) to the skillet, along with the dried mixed herbs. Bring the mixture to a simmer and let it cook for 5-7 minutes, stirring occasionally, until the sauce has thickened slightly.
6. Return the cooked kangaroo meat to the skillet and stir to combine. Cook for another 2-3 minutes to heat through.
7. Season the sauce with salt and pepper to taste.
8. Add the cooked pasta to the skillet with the kangaroo and tomato sauce. Toss everything together until the pasta is evenly coated with the sauce.
9. Serve the Kangaroo and Bush Tomato Pasta hot, garnished with grated Parmesan cheese and fresh basil leaves, if desired.
10. Enjoy your delicious and hearty Kangaroo and Bush Tomato Pasta!

Grilled Saltbush Lamb Chops

Ingredients:

- 8 lamb loin chops
- 2 tablespoons olive oil
- 2 tablespoons chopped fresh saltbush leaves (or dried saltbush, rehydrated)
- 2 cloves garlic, minced
- 1 teaspoon dried rosemary
- 1 teaspoon dried thyme
- Salt and pepper to taste

Instructions:

1. Preheat your grill to medium-high heat.
2. In a small bowl, combine the olive oil, chopped fresh saltbush leaves (or rehydrated dried saltbush), minced garlic, dried rosemary, dried thyme, salt, and pepper. Mix well to create a marinade.
3. Place the lamb chops in a shallow dish and pour the marinade over them, ensuring that each chop is coated evenly. Massage the marinade into the meat.
4. Allow the lamb chops to marinate for at least 30 minutes at room temperature, or for up to 4 hours in the refrigerator for maximum flavor.
5. Once marinated, remove the lamb chops from the dish and discard any excess marinade.
6. Place the lamb chops on the preheated grill and cook for about 3-4 minutes per side for medium-rare, or longer according to your preference. Cooking time will depend on the thickness of the chops and the desired level of doneness.
7. Avoid pressing down on the lamb chops with a spatula while grilling to retain their juices.
8. Once the lamb chops are cooked to your liking, remove them from the grill and let them rest for a few minutes before serving.
9. Serve the Grilled Saltbush Lamb Chops hot, garnished with additional fresh saltbush leaves if desired.
10. Enjoy your flavorful and tender Grilled Saltbush Lamb Chops as a main course, accompanied by your favorite sides!

Lemon Myrtle and Pepperberry Crusted Barramundi

Ingredients:

- 4 barramundi fillets
- 2 tablespoons lemon myrtle leaves, finely chopped
- 1 tablespoon ground pepperberry
- 1/2 cup breadcrumbs
- 2 tablespoons olive oil
- Salt and pepper to taste
- Lemon wedges for serving
- Fresh herbs for garnish (optional)

Instructions:

1. Preheat your oven to 200°C (400°F). Line a baking sheet with parchment paper or lightly grease it with olive oil.
2. In a shallow dish, combine the chopped lemon myrtle leaves, ground pepperberry, breadcrumbs, olive oil, salt, and pepper. Mix well to create the crust mixture.
3. Pat the barramundi fillets dry with paper towels. Season both sides of the fillets with salt and pepper.
4. Press each barramundi fillet into the crust mixture, coating both sides evenly. Gently press the crust onto the fillets to help it adhere.
5. Place the coated barramundi fillets on the prepared baking sheet.
6. Bake the barramundi fillets in the preheated oven for 12-15 minutes, or until the crust is golden brown and the fish is cooked through. Cooking time may vary depending on the thickness of the fillets.
7. Once cooked, remove the barramundi fillets from the oven and let them rest for a few minutes.
8. Serve the Lemon Myrtle and Pepperberry Crusted Barramundi hot, garnished with lemon wedges and fresh herbs if desired.
9. Enjoy your flavorful and aromatic barramundi fillets as a delicious and nutritious meal!

Wattleseed Pancakes with Native Honey

Ingredients:

For the Pancakes:

- 1 cup all-purpose flour
- 2 tablespoons wattleseed powder
- 2 tablespoons sugar
- 1 teaspoon baking powder
- 1/2 teaspoon baking soda
- 1/4 teaspoon salt
- 1 cup buttermilk
- 1 large egg
- 2 tablespoons unsalted butter, melted
- Butter or oil for cooking

For Serving:

- Native honey (such as Australian bush honey or manuka honey)
- Fresh berries or sliced fruits (optional)
- Whipped cream or yogurt (optional)

Instructions:

1. In a large mixing bowl, whisk together the all-purpose flour, wattleseed powder, sugar, baking powder, baking soda, and salt.
2. In a separate bowl, whisk together the buttermilk, egg, and melted butter until well combined.
3. Pour the wet ingredients into the dry ingredients and stir until just combined. Be careful not to overmix; a few lumps in the batter are okay.
4. Let the batter rest for about 5-10 minutes while you preheat a non-stick skillet or griddle over medium heat. If necessary, lightly grease the skillet or griddle with butter or oil.
5. Once the skillet or griddle is hot, pour about 1/4 cup of batter onto the cooking surface for each pancake. Cook until bubbles form on the surface of the pancake and the edges begin to look set, about 2-3 minutes.
6. Carefully flip the pancakes with a spatula and cook for an additional 1-2 minutes on the other side, or until golden brown and cooked through.
7. Repeat with the remaining batter, adjusting the heat as needed to prevent burning.

8. Serve the wattleseed pancakes warm, drizzled with native honey and topped with fresh berries or sliced fruits, if desired. You can also serve them with a dollop of whipped cream or yogurt for extra indulgence.
9. Enjoy your delicious Wattleseed Pancakes with Native Honey as a delightful breakfast or brunch treat!

Bush Tomato and Quandong Salad

Ingredients:

- 2 cups mixed salad greens (such as baby spinach, arugula, and lettuce)
- 1/2 cup fresh quandong fruits, pitted and sliced
- 1/4 cup sun-dried bush tomatoes, chopped
- 1/4 cup toasted macadamia nuts, roughly chopped
- 2 tablespoons olive oil
- 1 tablespoon lemon juice
- 1 teaspoon honey
- Salt and pepper to taste

Instructions:

1. In a large mixing bowl, combine the mixed salad greens, sliced quandong fruits, chopped sun-dried bush tomatoes, and toasted macadamia nuts.
2. In a small bowl, whisk together the olive oil, lemon juice, honey, salt, and pepper to create the dressing.
3. Drizzle the dressing over the salad ingredients in the large mixing bowl.
4. Toss the salad gently to coat all the ingredients evenly with the dressing.
5. Taste and adjust the seasoning if necessary, adding more salt, pepper, or lemon juice to suit your preference.
6. Transfer the dressed Bush Tomato and Quandong Salad to a serving platter or individual salad bowls.
7. Serve the salad immediately as a refreshing and flavorful side dish, or as a light meal on its own.
8. Enjoy your Bush Tomato and Quandong Salad, showcasing the unique flavors of Australian bush ingredients!

Crocodile Caesar Salad

Ingredients:

For the Crocodile:

- 400g crocodile tail fillets, skin removed
- Salt and pepper to taste
- 2 tablespoons olive oil
- 1 clove garlic, minced
- 1 teaspoon lemon zest
- 1 teaspoon dried oregano
- 1 teaspoon paprika

For the Caesar Dressing:

- 1/2 cup mayonnaise
- 2 tablespoons grated Parmesan cheese
- 1 tablespoon lemon juice
- 1 teaspoon Dijon mustard
- 1 clove garlic, minced
- Salt and pepper to taste

For the Salad:

- 1 large head of romaine lettuce, washed and chopped
- 1 cup croutons
- Grated Parmesan cheese for garnish

Instructions:

1. Preheat your grill or grill pan to medium-high heat.
2. Season the crocodile tail fillets with salt and pepper on both sides.
3. In a small bowl, mix together the olive oil, minced garlic, lemon zest, dried oregano, and paprika to make a marinade. Brush the marinade over the crocodile fillets, coating them evenly.
4. Grill the crocodile fillets for 3-4 minutes on each side, or until cooked through and grill marks appear. Cooking time may vary depending on the thickness of the fillets. Once cooked, remove from the grill and let them rest for a few minutes before slicing into thin strips.

5. While the crocodile is cooking, prepare the Caesar dressing. In a small bowl, whisk together the mayonnaise, grated Parmesan cheese, lemon juice, Dijon mustard, minced garlic, salt, and pepper until smooth and well combined. Adjust the seasoning to taste.
6. In a large salad bowl, combine the chopped romaine lettuce and croutons.
7. Add the sliced crocodile fillets to the salad bowl.
8. Drizzle the Caesar dressing over the salad, tossing gently to coat all the ingredients evenly with the dressing.
9. Transfer the Caesar Salad to serving plates or bowls, garnishing with additional grated Parmesan cheese if desired.
10. Serve immediately as a delicious and satisfying main course or appetizer.
11. Enjoy your flavorful Crocodile Caesar Salad!

Emu Egg Salad with Wild Greens

Ingredients:

For the Salad:

- 4 cups mixed wild greens (such as dandelion greens, purslane, or wild rocket)
- 2 emu eggs
- 1/4 cup cherry tomatoes, halved
- 1/4 cup cucumber, sliced
- 1/4 cup radishes, thinly sliced
- 1/4 cup red onion, thinly sliced
- 1/4 cup mixed fresh herbs (such as parsley, cilantro, and chives), chopped
- Salt and pepper to taste

For the Dressing:

- 2 tablespoons extra virgin olive oil
- 1 tablespoon white wine vinegar or apple cider vinegar
- 1 teaspoon Dijon mustard
- 1 teaspoon honey
- Salt and pepper to taste

Instructions:

1. Wash and dry the mixed wild greens thoroughly. Place them in a large salad bowl.
2. Hard-boil the emu eggs: Place the emu eggs in a saucepan and cover them with cold water. Bring the water to a boil over high heat, then reduce the heat to medium-low and simmer for 8-10 minutes. Remove the eggs from the hot water and transfer them to a bowl of ice water to cool completely. Once cooled, peel the eggs and chop them into bite-sized pieces.
3. Add the chopped emu eggs, halved cherry tomatoes, sliced cucumber, sliced radishes, sliced red onion, and chopped fresh herbs to the salad bowl with the mixed wild greens.
4. In a small bowl, whisk together the extra virgin olive oil, white wine vinegar or apple cider vinegar, Dijon mustard, honey, salt, and pepper to make the dressing.

5. Drizzle the dressing over the salad ingredients in the bowl.
6. Toss the salad gently to coat all the ingredients evenly with the dressing.
7. Taste and adjust the seasoning if necessary, adding more salt, pepper, or vinegar to suit your preference.
8. Transfer the Emu Egg Salad with Wild Greens to serving plates or bowls.
9. Serve immediately as a refreshing and nutritious salad, perfect for a light meal or as a side dish.
10. Enjoy your flavorful and vibrant Emu Egg Salad with Wild Greens!

Bush Tomato and Pepperberry Potato Wedges

Ingredients:

- 4 large potatoes, washed and scrubbed
- 2 tablespoons olive oil
- 1 tablespoon ground bush tomato
- 1 teaspoon ground pepperberry
- 1 teaspoon garlic powder
- 1 teaspoon onion powder
- Salt and pepper to taste
- Chopped fresh parsley or chives for garnish (optional)

Instructions:

1. Preheat your oven to 220°C (425°F). Line a baking sheet with parchment paper or lightly grease it with olive oil.
2. Cut each potato into wedges by halving them lengthwise, then cutting each half into 2-3 wedges, depending on the size of the potato.
3. Place the potato wedges in a large bowl. Drizzle the olive oil over the wedges and toss to coat evenly.
4. In a small bowl, mix together the ground bush tomato, ground pepperberry, garlic powder, onion powder, salt, and pepper.
5. Sprinkle the spice mixture over the potato wedges and toss until the wedges are evenly coated with the spices.
6. Arrange the seasoned potato wedges in a single layer on the prepared baking sheet.
7. Bake in the preheated oven for 25-30 minutes, flipping halfway through, or until the potato wedges are golden brown and crispy on the outside, and tender on the inside.
8. Once cooked, remove the potato wedges from the oven and transfer them to a serving platter.
9. Garnish the Bush Tomato and Pepperberry Potato Wedges with chopped fresh parsley or chives, if desired.
10. Serve hot as a delicious and flavorful side dish or snack.
11. Enjoy your tasty Bush Tomato and Pepperberry Potato Wedges!

Lemon Myrtle and Macadamia Nut Crusted Chicken Breast

Ingredients:

For the Chicken:

- 4 boneless, skinless chicken breasts
- Salt and pepper to taste
- 2 tablespoons olive oil

For the Crust:

- 1 cup macadamia nuts, finely chopped
- 2 tablespoons lemon myrtle leaves, finely chopped
- 1/4 cup breadcrumbs
- 1 tablespoon lemon zest
- 1 teaspoon garlic powder
- 1 teaspoon paprika
- Salt and pepper to taste

For the Lemon Butter Sauce (optional):

- 2 tablespoons unsalted butter
- 2 tablespoons lemon juice
- 1 tablespoon chopped fresh parsley (optional)

Instructions:

1. Preheat your oven to 200°C (400°F). Line a baking sheet with parchment paper or lightly grease it with olive oil.
2. Season the chicken breasts with salt and pepper on both sides.
3. In a shallow dish, combine the finely chopped macadamia nuts, lemon myrtle leaves, breadcrumbs, lemon zest, garlic powder, paprika, salt, and pepper to create the crust mixture.
4. Brush each chicken breast with olive oil, then coat them evenly with the crust mixture, pressing gently to adhere.
5. Place the coated chicken breasts on the prepared baking sheet.
6. Bake in the preheated oven for 20-25 minutes, or until the chicken is cooked through and the crust is golden brown and crispy.

7. While the chicken is baking, you can prepare the optional lemon butter sauce: In a small saucepan, melt the butter over medium heat. Stir in the lemon juice and chopped parsley (if using). Cook for 1-2 minutes, stirring occasionally, until heated through.
8. Once the chicken is cooked, remove it from the oven and let it rest for a few minutes.
9. Serve the Lemon Myrtle and Macadamia Nut Crusted Chicken Breast hot, drizzled with the optional lemon butter sauce if desired.
10. Enjoy your flavorful and aromatic chicken breasts, paired perfectly with the crunchy crust and hint of lemon myrtle!

Kangaroo and Wild Rice Pilaf

Ingredients:

- 1 cup wild rice
- 2 cups water or chicken broth
- 400g kangaroo meat, diced
- 1 tablespoon olive oil
- 1 onion, finely chopped
- 2 cloves garlic, minced
- 1 carrot, diced
- 1 celery stalk, diced
- 1 red bell pepper, diced
- 1/4 cup dried cranberries or raisins
- 1/4 cup chopped almonds or pecans
- 2 tablespoons chopped fresh parsley
- Salt and pepper to taste

Instructions:

1. Rinse the wild rice under cold water. In a saucepan, combine the wild rice and water or chicken broth. Bring to a boil over high heat, then reduce the heat to low, cover, and simmer for 45-50 minutes, or until the rice is tender and has absorbed the liquid. Remove from heat and let it sit, covered, for 5-10 minutes before fluffing with a fork.
2. While the rice is cooking, heat the olive oil in a large skillet over medium-high heat. Add the diced kangaroo meat and cook for 3-4 minutes, or until browned on all sides. Remove the kangaroo meat from the skillet and set aside.
3. In the same skillet, add the chopped onion and minced garlic. Cook for 2-3 minutes, or until the onion is translucent and fragrant.
4. Add the diced carrot, celery, and red bell pepper to the skillet. Cook for an additional 5-7 minutes, or until the vegetables are tender-crisp.
5. Return the cooked kangaroo meat to the skillet. Stir in the cooked wild rice, dried cranberries or raisins, chopped almonds or pecans, and chopped fresh parsley. Season with salt and pepper to taste.
6. Cook, stirring occasionally, for another 2-3 minutes, or until everything is heated through and well combined.
7. Remove the skillet from heat and serve the Kangaroo and Wild Rice Pilaf hot as a flavorful and nutritious main dish.
8. Enjoy your delicious and hearty Kangaroo and Wild Rice Pilaf, perfect for a satisfying meal!

Bush Tomato and Warrigal Greens Soup

Ingredients:

- 2 tablespoons olive oil
- 1 onion, chopped
- 2 cloves garlic, minced
- 2 cups warrigal greens, washed and chopped (substitute with spinach or kale if unavailable)
- 2 tablespoons dried bush tomato, chopped
- 4 cups vegetable or chicken broth
- 1 potato, peeled and diced
- 1 carrot, peeled and diced
- 1 celery stalk, diced
- Salt and pepper to taste
- Optional garnish: fresh parsley, croutons, or a dollop of yogurt

Instructions:

1. Heat the olive oil in a large pot over medium heat. Add the chopped onion and minced garlic, and sauté until softened and fragrant, about 2-3 minutes.
2. Add the chopped warrigal greens and dried bush tomato to the pot. Cook, stirring occasionally, for another 2-3 minutes.
3. Pour in the vegetable or chicken broth, and add the diced potato, carrot, and celery to the pot. Bring the mixture to a boil, then reduce the heat to low and let it simmer, covered, for about 20-25 minutes, or until the vegetables are tender.
4. Once the vegetables are cooked, use an immersion blender to puree the soup until smooth. Alternatively, transfer the soup in batches to a blender and blend until smooth, then return it to the pot.
5. Season the soup with salt and pepper to taste. Adjust the seasoning as needed.
6. If the soup is too thick, you can add more broth or water to reach your desired consistency.
7. Ladle the Bush Tomato and Warrigal Greens Soup into bowls. Garnish with fresh parsley, croutons, or a dollop of yogurt if desired.
8. Serve the soup hot as a comforting and nutritious meal.
9. Enjoy your flavorful and aromatic Bush Tomato and Warrigal Greens Soup!

Grilled Crocodile Skewers with Lemon Asparagus

Ingredients:

For the Crocodile Skewers:

- 500g crocodile meat, cut into chunks
- Wooden or metal skewers, soaked in water if wooden
- 2 tablespoons olive oil
- 2 cloves garlic, minced
- 1 teaspoon paprika
- 1 teaspoon ground cumin
- Salt and pepper to taste

For the Lemon Asparagus:

- 1 bunch asparagus, woody ends trimmed
- Zest and juice of 1 lemon
- 2 tablespoons olive oil
- Salt and pepper to taste

Instructions:

1. Preheat your grill to medium-high heat.
2. Thread the crocodile meat onto the skewers, distributing them evenly.
3. In a small bowl, mix together the olive oil, minced garlic, paprika, ground cumin, salt, and pepper to create a marinade.
4. Brush the marinade over the crocodile skewers, coating them evenly on all sides.
5. Place the skewers on the preheated grill and cook for about 3-4 minutes per side, or until the crocodile meat is cooked through and has nice grill marks. Cooking time may vary depending on the thickness of the meat.
6. While the crocodile skewers are grilling, prepare the lemon asparagus. In a shallow dish, combine the olive oil, lemon zest, lemon juice, salt, and pepper. Toss the trimmed asparagus in the lemon mixture to coat evenly.
7. Place the lemon-coated asparagus directly on the grill alongside the crocodile skewers. Grill for 2-3 minutes per side, or until the asparagus is tender and lightly charred.
8. Once the crocodile skewers and asparagus are cooked, remove them from the grill.
9. Serve the Grilled Crocodile Skewers with Lemon Asparagus hot as a delicious and unique main dish.
10. Enjoy your flavorful and nutritious meal with a touch of citrusy freshness!

Lemon Myrtle and Pepperberry Crumbed Fish Nuggets

Ingredients:

For the Fish Nuggets:

- 500g white fish fillets (such as cod or haddock), cut into bite-sized pieces
- 1 cup all-purpose flour
- 2 eggs, beaten
- 1 cup breadcrumbs
- 2 tablespoons lemon myrtle leaves, finely chopped
- 1 tablespoon ground pepperberry
- Salt and pepper to taste
- Vegetable oil for frying

For the Lemon Dipping Sauce:

- 1/2 cup mayonnaise
- 2 tablespoons lemon juice
- 1 teaspoon lemon zest
- 1 teaspoon honey
- Salt and pepper to taste

Instructions:

1. In a shallow dish, combine the all-purpose flour with a pinch of salt and pepper. In another shallow dish, place the beaten eggs. In a third shallow dish, mix together the breadcrumbs, chopped lemon myrtle leaves, ground pepperberry, and a pinch of salt and pepper.
2. Take each piece of fish and dredge it first in the flour mixture, shaking off any excess. Then dip it into the beaten eggs, ensuring it is coated evenly. Finally, coat the fish in the breadcrumb mixture, pressing gently to adhere. Place the coated fish nuggets on a plate or baking sheet.
3. Heat vegetable oil in a large skillet over medium-high heat. Once the oil is hot, carefully add the coated fish nuggets in batches, making sure not to overcrowd the pan. Fry the nuggets for 2-3 minutes on each side, or until golden brown and crispy. Transfer the cooked nuggets to a plate lined with paper towels to drain excess oil.
4. While the fish nuggets are frying, prepare the lemon dipping sauce. In a small bowl, whisk together the mayonnaise, lemon juice, lemon zest, honey, salt, and pepper until smooth and well combined. Adjust the seasoning to taste.

5. Once all the fish nuggets are cooked, serve them hot with the lemon dipping sauce on the side for dipping.
6. Enjoy your delicious and flavorful Lemon Myrtle and Pepperberry Crumbed Fish Nuggets as a tasty appetizer or main dish!

Kangaroo Meat Pie with Bush Tomato Gravy

Ingredients:

For the Kangaroo Filling:

- 500g kangaroo meat, diced
- 2 tablespoons olive oil
- 1 onion, finely chopped
- 2 cloves garlic, minced
- 2 carrots, diced
- 2 celery stalks, diced
- 2 tablespoons plain flour
- 2 cups beef or vegetable broth
- 2 tablespoons Worcestershire sauce
- 2 tablespoons tomato paste
- 1 teaspoon dried thyme
- Salt and pepper to taste

For the Bush Tomato Gravy:

- 1 tablespoon butter
- 1 tablespoon plain flour
- 1 cup beef or vegetable broth
- 2 tablespoons bush tomato chutney or bush tomato paste
- Salt and pepper to taste

For the Pie Crust:

- Store-bought puff pastry sheets, thawed
- 1 egg, beaten (for egg wash)

Instructions:

1. Preheat your oven to 200°C (400°F).

2. In a large skillet or saucepan, heat the olive oil over medium heat. Add the diced kangaroo meat and cook until browned on all sides. Remove the kangaroo meat from the skillet and set aside.
3. In the same skillet, add the chopped onion and minced garlic. Cook until softened and fragrant, about 2-3 minutes.
4. Add the diced carrots and celery to the skillet. Cook for another 5 minutes, or until the vegetables are tender.
5. Sprinkle the plain flour over the cooked vegetables in the skillet. Stir well to coat the vegetables with the flour.
6. Gradually pour in the beef or vegetable broth, stirring constantly to avoid lumps. Add the Worcestershire sauce, tomato paste, dried thyme, salt, and pepper. Stir to combine.
7. Return the cooked kangaroo meat to the skillet. Bring the mixture to a simmer and cook for 10-15 minutes, or until the filling has thickened. Remove from heat and let it cool slightly.
8. While the filling is cooling, prepare the bush tomato gravy. In a small saucepan, melt the butter over medium heat. Stir in the plain flour to form a roux. Cook for 1-2 minutes, stirring constantly.
9. Gradually whisk in the beef or vegetable broth until smooth. Add the bush tomato chutney or paste, salt, and pepper. Cook, stirring occasionally, until the gravy thickens to your desired consistency. Remove from heat and set aside.
10. Roll out the thawed puff pastry sheets on a lightly floured surface. Cut out circles large enough to fit the base and top of your pie dishes.
11. Line the base of each pie dish with one of the puff pastry circles. Spoon the kangaroo filling into the pie dishes, dividing it evenly among them.
12. Place the remaining puff pastry circles over the top of each pie dish. Seal the edges by pressing them together with a fork. Trim any excess pastry around the edges.
13. Brush the tops of the pies with beaten egg to create a golden crust.
14. Use a small knife to make a few slits in the top of each pie to allow steam to escape during baking.
15. Place the pies on a baking sheet lined with parchment paper and bake in the preheated oven for 25-30 minutes, or until the pastry is golden brown and cooked through.
16. Serve the Kangaroo Meat Pies hot, accompanied by the bush tomato gravy on the side.
17. Enjoy your delicious and hearty Kangaroo Meat Pies with Bush Tomato Gravy!

Outback Veggie Stir-Fry with Wattleseed Tofu

Ingredients:

For the Wattleseed Tofu:

- 400g firm tofu, pressed and cubed
- 2 tablespoons wattleseed powder
- 2 tablespoons soy sauce
- 1 tablespoon olive oil

For the Stir-Fry:

- 2 tablespoons olive oil
- 1 onion, thinly sliced
- 2 cloves garlic, minced
- 2 carrots, julienned
- 1 red bell pepper, thinly sliced
- 1 yellow bell pepper, thinly sliced
- 1 cup broccoli florets
- 1 cup snow peas, trimmed
- 1 cup sliced mushrooms
- 2 tablespoons soy sauce
- 1 tablespoon hoisin sauce
- 1 tablespoon rice vinegar
- 1 teaspoon sesame oil
- Salt and pepper to taste
- Cooked rice or noodles for serving

Instructions:

1. Preheat your oven to 200°C (400°F).
2. In a bowl, mix together the wattleseed powder and soy sauce to create a marinade. Add the cubed tofu to the marinade and toss gently to coat. Let it marinate for about 15-20 minutes.
3. Place the marinated tofu cubes on a baking sheet lined with parchment paper. Drizzle with olive oil. Bake in the preheated oven for 20-25 minutes, or until the tofu is golden brown and crispy on the outside.
4. While the tofu is baking, heat 2 tablespoons of olive oil in a large skillet or wok over medium-high heat. Add the thinly sliced onion and minced garlic. Stir-fry for 1-2 minutes until fragrant.

5. Add the julienned carrots, thinly sliced red and yellow bell peppers, broccoli florets, snow peas, and sliced mushrooms to the skillet. Stir-fry for another 5-6 minutes, or until the vegetables are tender-crisp.
6. In a small bowl, whisk together the soy sauce, hoisin sauce, rice vinegar, sesame oil, salt, and pepper. Pour the sauce over the stir-fried vegetables and tofu in the skillet.
7. Add the baked wattleseed tofu cubes to the skillet with the vegetables and sauce. Gently toss everything together until evenly coated with the sauce.
8. Cook for an additional 1-2 minutes, or until the sauce has thickened slightly and everything is heated through.
9. Remove from heat and serve the Outback Veggie Stir-Fry with Wattleseed Tofu hot, accompanied by cooked rice or noodles.
10. Enjoy your flavorful and nutritious stir-fry with a unique Australian twist!

Lemon Myrtle and Pepperberry Roast Chicken

Ingredients:

- 1 whole chicken (about 1.5-2 kg)
- 2 tablespoons olive oil
- 2 tablespoons lemon myrtle leaves, finely chopped
- 1 tablespoon ground pepperberry
- 1 teaspoon garlic powder
- 1 teaspoon paprika
- Salt and pepper to taste
- 1 lemon, sliced (optional)
- Fresh herbs for garnish (optional)

Instructions:

1. Preheat your oven to 200°C (400°F).
2. Rinse the chicken inside and out under cold water, then pat dry with paper towels.
3. In a small bowl, combine the olive oil, chopped lemon myrtle leaves, ground pepperberry, garlic powder, paprika, salt, and pepper to create a rub.
4. Rub the olive oil mixture all over the surface of the chicken, making sure to coat it evenly.
5. If desired, place a few slices of lemon inside the cavity of the chicken for added flavor.
6. Tie the legs of the chicken together with kitchen twine and tuck the wings under the body.
7. Place the chicken on a rack in a roasting pan, breast side up.
8. Roast the chicken in the preheated oven for about 1 hour to 1 hour 15 minutes, or until the internal temperature reaches 75°C (165°F) and the juices run clear when pierced with a knife between the leg and thigh.
9. If the skin starts to brown too quickly, you can cover the chicken loosely with foil halfway through cooking.
10. Once the chicken is cooked through, remove it from the oven and let it rest for about 10 minutes before carving.
11. Garnish with fresh herbs, if desired, before serving.
12. Carve the Lemon Myrtle and Pepperberry Roast Chicken and serve hot with your favorite side dishes.
13. Enjoy your flavorful and aromatic roast chicken with a unique Australian twist!

Bush Tomato and Pepperberry Lamb Kebabs

Ingredients:

- 500g lamb meat, cubed
- 2 tablespoons olive oil
- 2 tablespoons bush tomato chutney or paste
- 1 tablespoon ground pepperberry
- 2 cloves garlic, minced
- 1 tablespoon fresh rosemary, chopped
- Salt and pepper to taste
- Wooden or metal skewers, soaked in water if wooden
- Lemon wedges for serving (optional)

Instructions:

1. In a bowl, combine the olive oil, bush tomato chutney or paste, ground pepperberry, minced garlic, chopped fresh rosemary, salt, and pepper. Mix well to form a marinade.
2. Add the cubed lamb meat to the marinade, tossing to coat evenly. Cover the bowl and let the lamb marinate in the refrigerator for at least 1 hour, or preferably overnight for the flavors to develop.
3. Preheat your grill or barbecue to medium-high heat.
4. Thread the marinated lamb cubes onto the skewers, dividing them evenly among the skewers.
5. Place the lamb skewers on the preheated grill or barbecue. Cook for 3-4 minutes on each side, or until the lamb is cooked to your desired level of doneness and has nice grill marks.
6. Once cooked, remove the lamb kebabs from the grill and transfer them to a serving platter.
7. Serve the Bush Tomato and Pepperberry Lamb Kebabs hot, garnished with lemon wedges if desired.
8. Enjoy your flavorful and aromatic lamb kebabs, perfect for a barbecue or outdoor gathering!

Emu Egg Frittata with Bush Herbs

Ingredients:

- 6 emu eggs (or substitute with chicken eggs)
- 1/4 cup milk or cream
- 1 tablespoon olive oil
- 1 onion, finely chopped
- 2 cloves garlic, minced
- 1 cup mixed bush herbs (such as saltbush, warrigal greens, or lemon myrtle), chopped
- Salt and pepper to taste
- 1/2 cup grated cheese (optional)
- Fresh herbs for garnish (optional)

Instructions:

1. Preheat your oven to 180°C (350°F).
2. In a large bowl, whisk together the emu eggs and milk or cream until well combined. Season with salt and pepper to taste. Set aside.
3. Heat the olive oil in an oven-safe skillet over medium heat. Add the chopped onion and minced garlic, and sauté until softened and fragrant, about 2-3 minutes.
4. Add the chopped bush herbs to the skillet and cook for another 2-3 minutes, or until wilted.
5. Pour the emu egg mixture over the cooked herbs in the skillet. Gently stir to distribute the herbs evenly throughout the egg mixture.
6. Cook the frittata on the stovetop for 3-4 minutes, or until the edges begin to set.
7. Sprinkle the grated cheese evenly over the top of the frittata, if using.
8. Transfer the skillet to the preheated oven and bake for 12-15 minutes, or until the frittata is set in the center and lightly golden on top.
9. Once cooked, remove the frittata from the oven and let it cool slightly in the skillet.
10. Garnish with fresh herbs, if desired, before slicing and serving.
11. Serve the Emu Egg Frittata with Bush Herbs hot or at room temperature as a delicious and nutritious breakfast, brunch, or light meal.
12. Enjoy your flavorful and unique frittata showcasing Australian bush herbs!

Grilled Saltbush Lamb Rack with Mint Sauce

Ingredients:

For the Grilled Saltbush Lamb Rack:

- 1 rack of saltbush lamb, trimmed and frenched
- 2 tablespoons olive oil
- 2 cloves garlic, minced
- 1 tablespoon chopped fresh rosemary
- Salt and pepper to taste

For the Mint Sauce:

- 1/2 cup fresh mint leaves, finely chopped
- 2 tablespoons white wine vinegar
- 1 tablespoon honey
- 2 tablespoons olive oil
- Salt and pepper to taste

Instructions:

1. Preheat your grill to medium-high heat.
2. In a small bowl, mix together the olive oil, minced garlic, chopped fresh rosemary, salt, and pepper to create a marinade.
3. Place the saltbush lamb rack in a shallow dish and rub the marinade all over the meat, coating it evenly. Let it marinate for at least 30 minutes, or preferably overnight in the refrigerator.
4. While the lamb is marinating, prepare the mint sauce. In a small bowl, combine the finely chopped mint leaves, white wine vinegar, honey, olive oil, salt, and pepper. Mix well and set aside.
5. Once the lamb has finished marinating, remove it from the dish and let any excess marinade drip off.
6. Place the lamb rack on the preheated grill and cook for about 4-5 minutes per side for medium-rare, or longer according to your preference, turning occasionally to ensure even cooking.
7. Once the lamb is cooked to your desired doneness, remove it from the grill and let it rest for a few minutes before slicing.
8. Slice the Grilled Saltbush Lamb Rack into individual chops and arrange them on a serving platter.

9. Drizzle the mint sauce over the lamb chops or serve it on the side as a dipping sauce.
10. Garnish with fresh mint leaves, if desired, before serving.
11. Serve the Grilled Saltbush Lamb Rack with Mint Sauce hot as a delicious and flavorful main dish.
12. Enjoy your succulent and aromatic lamb chops with the refreshing mint sauce!

Lemon Myrtle and Bush Tomato Risotto

Ingredients:

- 1 cup Arborio rice
- 4 cups vegetable or chicken broth
- 2 tablespoons olive oil
- 1 onion, finely chopped
- 2 cloves garlic, minced
- 1 tablespoon lemon myrtle leaves, finely chopped
- 1 tablespoon bush tomato chutney or paste
- 1/4 cup white wine (optional)
- 1/2 cup grated Parmesan cheese
- Salt and pepper to taste
- Fresh parsley for garnish (optional)

Instructions:

1. In a saucepan, heat the vegetable or chicken broth over medium heat. Keep it warm but not boiling.
2. In a separate large skillet or saucepan, heat the olive oil over medium heat. Add the chopped onion and minced garlic, and sauté until softened and translucent, about 2-3 minutes.
3. Add the Arborio rice to the skillet and toast it for 1-2 minutes, stirring constantly, until the rice grains are coated with oil and slightly translucent.
4. Stir in the chopped lemon myrtle leaves and bush tomato chutney or paste, and cook for another minute to release their flavors.
5. If using white wine, pour it into the skillet and stir continuously until the wine is absorbed by the rice.
6. Begin adding the warm broth to the skillet, one ladleful at a time, stirring constantly and allowing each addition to be absorbed before adding more. Continue this process until the rice is creamy and tender, but still slightly firm to the bite (al dente), about 18-20 minutes.
7. Stir in the grated Parmesan cheese until melted and well combined. Season with salt and pepper to taste.
8. Remove the risotto from heat and let it rest for a minute or two.
9. Serve the Lemon Myrtle and Bush Tomato Risotto hot, garnished with fresh parsley if desired.
10. Enjoy your creamy and aromatic risotto, infused with the flavors of lemon myrtle and bush tomato!

Bush Tomato and Pepperberry Beef Stir-Fry

Ingredients:

For the Stir-Fry:

- 500g beef sirloin or flank steak, thinly sliced against the grain
- 2 tablespoons olive oil
- 1 onion, thinly sliced
- 2 bell peppers (red, green, or yellow), thinly sliced
- 1 cup sliced mushrooms
- 2 cloves garlic, minced
- 1 tablespoon bush tomato chutney or paste
- 1 tablespoon ground pepperberry
- Salt and pepper to taste
- Cooked rice or noodles for serving

For the Sauce:

- 1/4 cup soy sauce
- 2 tablespoons oyster sauce
- 1 tablespoon hoisin sauce
- 1 tablespoon rice vinegar
- 1 teaspoon sesame oil
- 1 teaspoon cornstarch

Instructions:

1. In a small bowl, whisk together all the ingredients for the sauce: soy sauce, oyster sauce, hoisin sauce, rice vinegar, sesame oil, and cornstarch. Set aside.
2. Heat 1 tablespoon of olive oil in a large skillet or wok over high heat. Add the thinly sliced beef and stir-fry for 2-3 minutes, or until browned. Remove the beef from the skillet and set aside.
3. In the same skillet, heat the remaining tablespoon of olive oil. Add the thinly sliced onion and bell peppers, and cook for 2-3 minutes, or until slightly softened.

4. Add the sliced mushrooms and minced garlic to the skillet, and continue to stir-fry for another 2-3 minutes, or until the vegetables are tender-crisp.
5. Return the cooked beef to the skillet. Stir in the bush tomato chutney or paste and ground pepperberry, mixing well to coat the beef and vegetables.
6. Pour the prepared sauce over the beef and vegetables in the skillet. Stir-fry for another 1-2 minutes, or until the sauce thickens and everything is heated through.
7. Season with salt and pepper to taste, if needed.
8. Remove the skillet from heat and serve the Bush Tomato and Pepperberry Beef Stir-Fry hot, accompanied by cooked rice or noodles.
9. Enjoy your flavorful and aromatic beef stir-fry with a unique Australian twist!
10. Optional: Garnish with chopped green onions or sesame seeds before serving, if desired.

Kangaroo and Wild Mushroom Pie

Ingredients:

For the Filling:

- 500g kangaroo meat, diced
- 200g wild mushrooms (such as shiitake, oyster, or porcini), sliced
- 1 onion, chopped
- 2 cloves garlic, minced
- 2 tablespoons olive oil
- 2 tablespoons plain flour
- 1 cup beef or vegetable broth
- 1/4 cup red wine (optional)
- 1 tablespoon Worcestershire sauce
- 1 tablespoon tomato paste
- 1 teaspoon dried thyme
- Salt and pepper to taste

For the Pastry:

- Store-bought puff pastry sheets, thawed
- 1 egg, beaten (for egg wash)

Instructions:

1. Preheat your oven to 200°C (400°F).
2. In a large skillet or saucepan, heat the olive oil over medium-high heat. Add the diced kangaroo meat and cook until browned on all sides. Remove the kangaroo meat from the skillet and set aside.
3. In the same skillet, add the chopped onion and minced garlic. Cook until softened and translucent, about 2-3 minutes.
4. Add the sliced wild mushrooms to the skillet and cook until they release their moisture and start to brown, about 5-7 minutes.
5. Sprinkle the plain flour over the cooked mushrooms and onions in the skillet. Stir well to coat the vegetables with the flour.
6. Gradually pour in the beef or vegetable broth, stirring constantly to avoid lumps. Add the red wine (if using), Worcestershire sauce, tomato paste, dried thyme, salt, and pepper. Stir to combine.

7. Return the cooked kangaroo meat to the skillet. Bring the mixture to a simmer and cook for 10-15 minutes, or until the filling has thickened. Remove from heat and let it cool slightly.
8. While the filling is cooling, prepare the puff pastry. Roll out the thawed puff pastry sheets on a lightly floured surface. Cut out circles large enough to fit the base and top of your pie dish or individual pie dishes.
9. Line the base of each pie dish with one of the puff pastry circles. Spoon the kangaroo and wild mushroom filling into the pie dishes, dividing it evenly among them.
10. Place the remaining puff pastry circles over the top of each pie dish. Seal the edges by pressing them together with a fork. Trim any excess pastry around the edges.
11. Brush the tops of the pies with beaten egg to create a golden crust.
12. Use a small knife to make a few slits in the top of each pie to allow steam to escape during baking.
13. Place the pies on a baking sheet lined with parchment paper and bake in the preheated oven for 25-30 minutes, or until the pastry is golden brown and cooked through.
14. Serve the Kangaroo and Wild Mushroom Pies hot as a delicious and hearty meal.
15. Enjoy your flavorful and aromatic pies, perfect for any occasion!

Outback Vegetable Curry with Wattleseed Rice

Ingredients:

For the Vegetable Curry:

- 2 tablespoons olive oil
- 1 onion, diced
- 2 cloves garlic, minced
- 1 tablespoon grated ginger
- 2 carrots, diced
- 2 potatoes, diced
- 1 sweet potato, diced
- 1 bell pepper (any color), diced
- 1 cup cauliflower florets
- 1 cup broccoli florets
- 1 cup green beans, trimmed and halved
- 1 can (400g) chickpeas, drained and rinsed
- 1 can (400g) diced tomatoes
- 1 can (400ml) coconut milk
- 2 tablespoons curry powder
- 1 teaspoon ground cumin
- 1 teaspoon ground coriander
- 1 teaspoon ground turmeric
- Salt and pepper to taste
- Fresh cilantro for garnish (optional)

For the Wattleseed Rice:

- 1 cup long-grain white rice
- 2 cups water
- 1 tablespoon wattleseed

Instructions:

For the Vegetable Curry:

1. Heat the olive oil in a large pot or Dutch oven over medium heat. Add the diced onion and cook until softened, about 5 minutes.

2. Add the minced garlic and grated ginger to the pot, and cook for another 1-2 minutes until fragrant.
3. Stir in the diced carrots, potatoes, sweet potato, and bell pepper. Cook for 5-7 minutes, stirring occasionally, until the vegetables start to soften.
4. Add the cauliflower florets, broccoli florets, and green beans to the pot. Cook for an additional 5 minutes.
5. Stir in the drained chickpeas, diced tomatoes, coconut milk, curry powder, ground cumin, ground coriander, and ground turmeric. Season with salt and pepper to taste.
6. Bring the curry to a simmer, then reduce the heat to low. Cover and let it simmer gently for about 20-25 minutes, stirring occasionally, until the vegetables are tender and the flavors have melded together.
7. While the curry is simmering, prepare the wattleseed rice.

For the Wattleseed Rice:

1. Rinse the white rice under cold water until the water runs clear. Drain well.
2. In a saucepan, combine the rinsed rice, water, and wattleseed. Bring to a boil over high heat.
3. Once boiling, reduce the heat to low, cover, and let it simmer for about 15-18 minutes, or until the rice is cooked and the water has been absorbed.
4. Remove the saucepan from the heat and let the rice sit, covered, for 5 minutes. Then fluff the rice with a fork.

To Serve:

1. Divide the wattleseed rice among serving plates or bowls.
2. Ladle the Outback Vegetable Curry over the wattleseed rice.
3. Garnish with fresh cilantro, if desired.
4. Serve hot and enjoy your flavorful and aromatic Outback Vegetable Curry with Wattleseed Rice!

Lemon Myrtle and Macadamia Crusted Snapper

Ingredients:

- 4 snapper fillets (about 150-200g each)
- 1/2 cup macadamia nuts, finely chopped
- 2 tablespoons lemon myrtle leaves, finely chopped
- 1/4 cup breadcrumbs
- 2 tablespoons olive oil
- Salt and pepper to taste
- Lemon wedges for serving

Instructions:

1. Preheat your oven to 200°C (400°F). Line a baking sheet with parchment paper or lightly grease it.
2. In a shallow dish, combine the chopped macadamia nuts, chopped lemon myrtle leaves, breadcrumbs, salt, and pepper. Mix well to combine.
3. Pat the snapper fillets dry with paper towels to remove any excess moisture.
4. Brush each snapper fillet with olive oil on both sides.
5. Press each snapper fillet into the macadamia and lemon myrtle mixture, coating it evenly on all sides. Press gently to adhere the crust to the fish.
6. Place the coated snapper fillets on the prepared baking sheet.
7. Bake in the preheated oven for 12-15 minutes, or until the fish is cooked through and the crust is golden brown and crispy.
8. Remove the baked snapper fillets from the oven and let them cool slightly for a few minutes.
9. Serve the Lemon Myrtle and Macadamia Crusted Snapper hot, garnished with lemon wedges.
10. Enjoy your flavorful and aromatic snapper fillets with a crunchy crust of lemon myrtle and macadamia nuts!

Bush Tomato and Pepperberry Kangaroo Sausages

Ingredients:

- 500g kangaroo meat, minced
- 1 tablespoon bush tomato chutney or paste
- 1 tablespoon ground pepperberry
- 1 teaspoon ground coriander
- 1 teaspoon ground cumin
- 1 teaspoon garlic powder
- 1 teaspoon onion powder
- Salt and pepper to taste
- Sausage casings (optional)

Instructions:

1. In a large mixing bowl, combine the minced kangaroo meat with the bush tomato chutney or paste, ground pepperberry, ground coriander, ground cumin, garlic powder, onion powder, salt, and pepper. Mix well to ensure the spices are evenly distributed throughout the meat.
2. If using sausage casings, soak them in cold water according to the package instructions.
3. If not using sausage casings, shape the seasoned kangaroo meat mixture into sausage patties or form them into sausage shapes.
4. If using sausage casings, thread the casings onto a sausage stuffer attachment on a sausage-making machine or onto a sausage funnel. Stuff the seasoned kangaroo meat mixture into the casings, tying them off into individual sausages of your desired length.
5. Once the sausages are formed, refrigerate them for at least 1 hour to allow the flavors to meld and the sausages to firm up.
6. Preheat your grill or barbecue to medium-high heat.
7. Grill the kangaroo sausages for about 5-7 minutes on each side, or until they are cooked through and have developed a nice char on the outside.
8. Alternatively, you can pan-fry the kangaroo sausages in a skillet over medium heat with a little olive oil for about 8-10 minutes, turning occasionally, until they are cooked through and evenly browned.
9. Once cooked, remove the kangaroo sausages from the grill or skillet and let them rest for a few minutes before serving.
10. Serve the Bush Tomato and Pepperberry Kangaroo Sausages hot, accompanied by your favorite sides or as part of a barbecue feast.
11. Enjoy your flavorful and uniquely Australian kangaroo sausages with the distinctive taste of bush tomato and pepperberry!

Crocodile Tail Soup with Lemon Myrtle Dumplings

Ingredients:

For the Crocodile Tail Soup:

- 500g crocodile tail meat, chopped into bite-sized pieces
- 2 tablespoons olive oil
- 1 onion, diced
- 2 carrots, diced
- 2 celery stalks, diced
- 2 cloves garlic, minced
- 1 bay leaf
- 6 cups chicken or vegetable broth
- Salt and pepper to taste
- Fresh parsley for garnish (optional)

For the Lemon Myrtle Dumplings:

- 1 cup all-purpose flour
- 1 teaspoon baking powder
- 1/4 teaspoon salt
- 1 tablespoon lemon myrtle leaves, finely chopped
- 2 tablespoons butter, melted
- 1/2 cup milk

Instructions:

For the Crocodile Tail Soup:

1. In a large pot or Dutch oven, heat the olive oil over medium heat. Add the diced onion, carrots, and celery. Cook until softened, about 5 minutes.
2. Add the minced garlic and chopped crocodile tail meat to the pot. Cook until the meat is browned on all sides.
3. Pour in the chicken or vegetable broth and add the bay leaf. Bring the soup to a simmer.
4. Reduce the heat to low and let the soup simmer gently for about 30-40 minutes, or until the crocodile tail meat is tender.
5. Season the soup with salt and pepper to taste.
6. While the soup is simmering, prepare the lemon myrtle dumplings.

For the Lemon Myrtle Dumplings:

1. In a mixing bowl, whisk together the flour, baking powder, salt, and chopped lemon myrtle leaves.
2. Add the melted butter and milk to the dry ingredients. Stir until just combined, being careful not to overmix.
3. Drop spoonfuls of the dumpling batter into the simmering soup, spacing them evenly apart.
4. Cover the pot and let the dumplings cook for about 15 minutes, or until they are puffed up and cooked through.
5. Once the dumplings are cooked, remove the pot from heat.
6. Ladle the Crocodile Tail Soup with Lemon Myrtle Dumplings into bowls. Garnish with fresh parsley if desired.
7. Serve hot and enjoy your unique and flavorful crocodile tail soup with lemon myrtle dumplings!
8. Note: Ensure the crocodile tail meat is cooked through before serving. Adjust the cooking time as needed based on the thickness of the meat pieces.

Kangaroo and Bush Tomato Lasagna

Ingredients:

For the Kangaroo Bolognese Sauce:

- 500g kangaroo mince
- 2 tablespoons olive oil
- 1 onion, finely chopped
- 2 cloves garlic, minced
- 1 carrot, finely chopped
- 1 celery stalk, finely chopped
- 1 red bell pepper, finely chopped
- 1 can (400g) crushed tomatoes
- 2 tablespoons bush tomato chutney or paste
- 1 teaspoon dried oregano
- 1 teaspoon dried basil
- Salt and pepper to taste

For the Cheese Sauce (Béchamel):

- 50g butter
- 1/4 cup all-purpose flour
- 2 cups milk
- 1 cup grated Parmesan cheese
- Salt and pepper to taste

For the Lasagna:

- 250g lasagna noodles (about 10-12 sheets), cooked according to package instructions
- 1 cup grated mozzarella cheese
- Fresh basil leaves for garnish (optional)

Instructions:

For the Kangaroo Bolognese Sauce:

1. Heat the olive oil in a large skillet or saucepan over medium heat. Add the chopped onion, minced garlic, chopped carrot, celery, and red bell pepper. Cook until softened, about 5-7 minutes.
2. Add the kangaroo mince to the skillet. Cook, breaking up the meat with a spoon, until browned and cooked through.
3. Stir in the crushed tomatoes, bush tomato chutney or paste, dried oregano, dried basil, salt, and pepper. Bring the sauce to a simmer and cook for about 15-20 minutes, stirring occasionally, until thickened. Remove from heat and set aside.

For the Cheese Sauce (Béchamel):

1. In a saucepan, melt the butter over medium heat. Once melted, add the flour and whisk continuously for 1-2 minutes to form a roux.
2. Gradually pour in the milk, whisking constantly to prevent lumps from forming.
3. Continue to cook the sauce, stirring frequently, until it thickens enough to coat the back of a spoon.
4. Remove the saucepan from the heat and stir in the grated Parmesan cheese until melted and smooth. Season with salt and pepper to taste. Set aside.

For Assembling the Lasagna:

1. Preheat your oven to 180°C (350°F).
2. Spread a thin layer of the kangaroo bolognese sauce on the bottom of a greased 9x13-inch baking dish.
3. Place a layer of cooked lasagna noodles on top of the sauce.
4. Spread a layer of the kangaroo bolognese sauce over the noodles, followed by a layer of the cheese sauce.
5. Repeat the layers of noodles, bolognese sauce, and cheese sauce until all ingredients are used, finishing with a layer of cheese sauce on top.
6. Sprinkle the grated mozzarella cheese evenly over the top of the lasagna.
7. Cover the baking dish with aluminum foil and bake in the preheated oven for 30 minutes.
8. Remove the foil and continue baking for an additional 10-15 minutes, or until the cheese is bubbly and golden brown.
9. Remove the lasagna from the oven and let it cool for a few minutes before serving.
10. Garnish with fresh basil leaves if desired.
11. Slice and serve the Kangaroo and Bush Tomato Lasagna hot, accompanied by a side salad or garlic bread if desired.
12. Enjoy your unique and flavorful kangaroo lasagna with bush tomato bolognese sauce!

Lemon Myrtle and Pepperberry Crusted Tuna Steak

Ingredients:

- 2 tuna steaks (about 200-250g each)
- 2 tablespoons olive oil
- 1 tablespoon lemon myrtle leaves, finely chopped
- 1 tablespoon ground pepperberry
- 1/4 cup breadcrumbs
- Salt and pepper to taste
- Lemon wedges for serving

Instructions:

1. Preheat your oven to 200°C (400°F). Line a baking sheet with parchment paper or lightly grease it.
2. In a small bowl, mix together the chopped lemon myrtle leaves, ground pepperberry, breadcrumbs, salt, and pepper.
3. Pat the tuna steaks dry with paper towels to remove any excess moisture.
4. Brush each tuna steak with olive oil on both sides.
5. Press each tuna steak into the lemon myrtle and pepperberry mixture, coating it evenly on all sides. Press gently to adhere the crust to the fish.
6. Place the coated tuna steaks on the prepared baking sheet.
7. Bake in the preheated oven for 8-10 minutes for medium-rare, or longer according to your preference, until the tuna is cooked to your desired level of doneness.
8. Once cooked, remove the tuna steaks from the oven and let them rest for a few minutes.
9. Serve the Lemon Myrtle and Pepperberry Crusted Tuna Steaks hot, accompanied by lemon wedges for squeezing over the top.
10. Enjoy your flavorful and aromatic tuna steaks with a unique Australian twist!
11. Optional: Serve with a side of steamed vegetables, rice, or salad for a complete meal.

Bush Tomato and Quandong Chutney

Ingredients:

- 1 cup dried quandong (native Australian fruit), chopped
- 1/2 cup bush tomato, chopped
- 1 onion, finely chopped
- 2 cloves garlic, minced
- 1/2 cup apple cider vinegar
- 1/2 cup brown sugar
- 1/2 teaspoon ground ginger
- 1/2 teaspoon ground cinnamon
- 1/4 teaspoon ground cloves
- 1/4 teaspoon ground nutmeg
- Salt to taste

Instructions:

1. In a medium saucepan, combine the chopped quandong, bush tomato, onion, garlic, apple cider vinegar, and brown sugar.
2. Place the saucepan over medium heat and bring the mixture to a simmer.
3. Reduce the heat to low and let the mixture cook gently for about 30-40 minutes, stirring occasionally, until the fruits are soft and the mixture has thickened.
4. Add the ground ginger, ground cinnamon, ground cloves, and ground nutmeg to the saucepan. Stir well to incorporate the spices.
5. Continue to cook the chutney for another 10-15 minutes, or until it reaches a thick, jam-like consistency.
6. Taste the chutney and adjust the seasoning with salt as needed.
7. Once the chutney is ready, remove the saucepan from the heat and let it cool slightly.
8. Transfer the bush tomato and quandong chutney to sterilized jars and seal tightly.
9. Allow the chutney to cool completely before storing it in the refrigerator.
10. Serve the Bush Tomato and Quandong Chutney as a condiment with cheese platters, cold meats, sandwiches, or as a delicious accompaniment to grilled meats or poultry.
11. Enjoy your unique and flavorful Australian chutney with the distinctive taste of bush tomato and quandong!

Emu Egg Benedict with Pepperberry Hollandaise

Ingredients:

For the Pepperberry Hollandaise Sauce:

- 3 large emu egg yolks
- 1 tablespoon lemon juice
- 1/2 cup unsalted butter, melted
- 1 teaspoon ground pepperberry
- Salt to taste

For the Emu Egg Benedict:

- 4 emu eggs (or substitute with chicken eggs)
- 4 English muffins, split and toasted
- 8 slices Canadian bacon or ham
- Salt and pepper to taste
- Fresh chives or parsley for garnish (optional)

Instructions:

For the Pepperberry Hollandaise Sauce:

1. Fill a saucepan with about 1 inch of water and bring it to a gentle simmer over medium heat.
2. In a heatproof bowl that fits snugly over the saucepan (double boiler), whisk together the emu egg yolks and lemon juice until well combined.
3. Place the bowl over the simmering water, making sure the bottom of the bowl doesn't touch the water.
4. Gradually whisk in the melted butter, a little at a time, until the sauce thickens and emulsifies.
5. Once all the butter has been incorporated and the sauce has thickened, remove the bowl from the heat.
6. Stir in the ground pepperberry and season with salt to taste. Keep the hollandaise warm while you prepare the rest of the dish, placing the bowl over a pot of warm water if needed.

For the Emu Egg Benedict:

1. Preheat your oven to a low setting to keep the cooked components warm while you prepare the rest of the dish.
2. In a large skillet, fry the Canadian bacon or ham slices until they are heated through and lightly browned. Remove them from the skillet and keep them warm in the oven.
3. Poach the emu eggs: Bring a large pot of water to a gentle simmer. Crack each emu egg into a small bowl or ramekin. Create a gentle whirlpool in the simmering water with a spoon and carefully slide each egg into the center. Poach for about 3-4 minutes, or until the egg whites are set but the yolks are still runny. Use a slotted spoon to remove the poached eggs from the water and drain them on paper towels.
4. Assemble the Emu Egg Benedict: Place a toasted English muffin half on each serving plate. Top each muffin half with a slice of Canadian bacon or ham, followed by a poached emu egg.
5. Spoon the warm Pepperberry Hollandaise Sauce over the top of each poached egg.
6. Garnish with freshly chopped chives or parsley, if desired.
7. Serve the Emu Egg Benedict immediately, while still warm.
8. Enjoy your unique and flavorful twist on the classic Eggs Benedict, featuring emu eggs and pepperberry hollandaise sauce!

Grilled Barramundi with Bush Tomato Salsa

Ingredients:

For the Grilled Barramundi:

- 4 barramundi fillets
- 2 tablespoons olive oil
- Salt and pepper to taste
- Lemon wedges for serving

For the Bush Tomato Salsa:

- 2 large ripe tomatoes, diced
- 2 tablespoons bush tomato, chopped
- 1/4 cup red onion, finely chopped
- 1/4 cup fresh cilantro (coriander), chopped
- 1 tablespoon lime juice
- 1 tablespoon olive oil
- Salt and pepper to taste

Instructions:

For the Grilled Barramundi:

1. Preheat your grill to medium-high heat.
2. Pat the barramundi fillets dry with paper towels. Drizzle olive oil over both sides of the fillets and season with salt and pepper.
3. Place the barramundi fillets on the preheated grill. Grill for about 4-5 minutes on each side, or until the fish is cooked through and easily flakes with a fork.
4. Once cooked, remove the barramundi fillets from the grill and transfer them to a serving platter.
5. Squeeze fresh lemon juice over the grilled barramundi fillets just before serving.

For the Bush Tomato Salsa:

1. In a medium bowl, combine the diced tomatoes, chopped bush tomato, finely chopped red onion, chopped fresh cilantro, lime juice, and olive oil.

2. Season the salsa with salt and pepper to taste. Mix well to combine all the ingredients.
3. Let the salsa sit for about 10 minutes to allow the flavors to meld together.
4. Serve the Grilled Barramundi with Bush Tomato Salsa spooned over the top or served on the side.
5. Garnish with additional fresh cilantro, if desired.
6. Enjoy your delicious and flavorful Grilled Barramundi with Bush Tomato Salsa!

Feel free to adjust the seasoning and ingredients according to your taste preferences.

Lemon Myrtle and Wattleseed Ice Cream

Ingredients:

- 2 cups heavy cream
- 1 cup whole milk
- 3/4 cup granulated sugar
- 4 large egg yolks
- 1 tablespoon lemon myrtle leaves, finely chopped
- 1 tablespoon wattleseed
- 1 teaspoon vanilla extract

Instructions:

1. In a medium saucepan, combine the heavy cream, whole milk, chopped lemon myrtle leaves, and wattleseed. Heat the mixture over medium heat until it just begins to simmer. Remove from heat and let it steep for about 30 minutes to infuse the flavors.
2. In a separate bowl, whisk together the egg yolks and granulated sugar until light and creamy.
3. After the cream mixture has finished steeping, reheat it over medium heat until it just starts to simmer again.
4. Slowly pour about 1/2 cup of the hot cream mixture into the bowl with the egg yolks, whisking constantly to temper the eggs.
5. Gradually pour the tempered egg mixture back into the saucepan with the remaining cream mixture, whisking constantly.
6. Cook the mixture over medium heat, stirring constantly with a wooden spoon or spatula, until it thickens slightly and coats the back of the spoon, about 5-7 minutes. Do not let it boil.
7. Once thickened, remove the saucepan from heat and strain the mixture through a fine-mesh sieve into a clean bowl to remove the lemon myrtle leaves and wattleseed.
8. Stir in the vanilla extract.
9. Cover the bowl with plastic wrap, pressing it directly onto the surface of the custard to prevent a skin from forming. Chill the custard in the refrigerator for at least 4 hours or overnight until completely cold.
10. Once chilled, churn the custard in an ice cream maker according to the manufacturer's instructions until it reaches a soft-serve consistency.
11. Transfer the churned ice cream to a freezer-safe container and freeze for at least 4 hours or until firm.
12. Serve the Lemon Myrtle and Wattleseed Ice Cream scooped into bowls or cones.
13. Enjoy your creamy and aromatic ice cream with the unique flavors of lemon myrtle and wattleseed!

Bush Tomato and Pepperberry Chocolate Brownies

Ingredients:

- 1/2 cup unsalted butter
- 1 cup granulated sugar
- 2 large eggs
- 1 teaspoon vanilla extract
- 1/3 cup unsweetened cocoa powder
- 1/2 cup all-purpose flour
- 1/4 teaspoon salt
- 1 teaspoon ground pepperberry
- 2 tablespoons bush tomato, finely chopped
- 1/2 cup semi-sweet chocolate chips

Instructions:

1. Preheat your oven to 350°F (175°C). Grease and flour an 8-inch square baking pan, or line it with parchment paper for easier removal.
2. In a medium saucepan, melt the butter over low heat. Remove from heat and let it cool slightly.
3. In a large mixing bowl, whisk together the melted butter and granulated sugar until well combined.
4. Add the eggs, one at a time, to the butter and sugar mixture, beating well after each addition.
5. Stir in the vanilla extract.
6. Sift in the cocoa powder, all-purpose flour, salt, and ground pepperberry. Mix until just combined.
7. Fold in the chopped bush tomato and semi-sweet chocolate chips until evenly distributed throughout the batter.
8. Pour the batter into the prepared baking pan and spread it out evenly with a spatula.
9. Bake in the preheated oven for 25-30 minutes, or until a toothpick inserted into the center comes out with moist crumbs, but not wet batter.
10. Remove the brownies from the oven and let them cool completely in the pan on a wire rack.
11. Once cooled, slice the brownies into squares or rectangles.
12. Serve the Bush Tomato and Pepperberry Chocolate Brownies as a delicious treat for dessert or as a snack.
13. Enjoy the unique combination of flavors in these indulgent brownies, perfect for any occasion!